CW00847293

Management
in 57 Minutes

LEADERSHIP ESSENTIALS FOR NEW MANAGERS

Mike Jackson and Pierre Lever

ISBN: 1508814864
ISBN 13: 9781508814863

Table of Contents

Deliver

WHAT THIS BOOK IS ABOUT

"...think of Management in 57 Minutes as your own management cheat sheet."

THE BEST LEARNING comes from experiencing successes you'd like to repeat and failures you'd like to forget. Although there are plenty of books available to help prepare you for these experiences, many of them are too theoretical and far too long.

Management in 57 Minutes is different.

This book was written specifically to provide first-time managers with practical leadership insights in a format that takes under an hour to read. We wrote it with one thought in mind: what do we wish we had known early on in our careers that would have given us the best possible start in management? We have drawn on over thirty years of collective experience in management and hundreds of hours of research to cover topics such as how to gain the trust of a new team, what to look for when hiring, when to deal with underperformers, where to focus your time and energy, what to do when you screw up, and many others.

Getting to grips with these topics will help you **inspire** your team to **deliver** results—the two hallmarks of every successful manager.

You should think of *Management in 57 Minutes* as your own management cheat sheet.

Our first book, *57 Minutes: All That Stands Between You and a Better Life*, was described by one of our readers as "*All meat and no bun.*" We like that description because it's exactly the goal of the *57 Minutes* guides. We want to share powerful, practical ideas that will help you without taking up more than an hour of your time.

Let's get started…

Inspire

EARN RESPECT, DON'T EXPECT IT

"....humility generates a respect all of its own."

WHEN YOU START out in your new management role, a good rule to remember is that respect is earned, not owed. Your goal is to help your team be as successful as possible, and to do this, you will need to gain their trust.

A good way to start gaining trust early is to embrace the leadership concept outlined by broadcasting executive Donald McGannon, who said: *"Leadership is an action, not a position."* Start by telling your team that you won't take anything for granted and that you recognize you'll need to work hard to demonstrate your value over time. There's nothing wrong with being confidently humble. In fact, this form of humility generates a respect all of its own.

Here are a few tips that we've used successfully to earn respect as managers.

Remember that your team already knows you're the boss. You don't need to remind the people who report to you that you're their boss—they know! Dictatorial expressions of firmness or threats to fire people if they don't do as you say are unnecessary. This type of management behavior results in resentment and disengagement—sometimes even defiance—and is rarely, if ever, effective for sustaining results. Rather, show appreciation for your team's ideas. Ask for their opinions. The act of seeking counsel from others makes them feel respected and more inclined to respect you back.

Provide a service to your team. Consider part of your role as a manager to be a service provider to the individual members of your team. This way, you will work to find every opportunity to add value to them early on, rather than always expecting they add value to you. In your one-on-one meetings with team members, dive down into the details of some of their concerns. Try and shape problems in a new light, as this can often help them find solutions on their own. Respect will gradually build if a team member feels that, with you, they reach answers faster and better than without you.

Say what you're going to do, and do what you say. Start your management career by keeping your promises, no matter how small. Delivering on your commitments is the best demonstration of your loyalty to your team, and it makes it easier for your team to respond in kind. Call when you said you would, show up to meetings on time, and implement the plan of action you said you would put in place. Making promises to your team—and keeping them—is an integral component of earning respect as a leader.

When I took on my first role as a general manager, the company I had inherited was in pretty rough shape. There was a severe lack of trust between the managers and the employees, and the customers were disillusioned about the service we were providing. My first task in resolving the company's difficulties was to find out what was going on and what options we had to sort them out.

I started by meeting with everyone in the company, both one-on-one and in groups. I made every effort to learn about the day-to-day struggles of my team and what they felt the potential solutions might be. I asked questions, I didn't assume that I knew the answers, and I didn't make threats. I also conducted an anonymous survey to get feedback that people may not have felt comfortable sharing with me in person.

Armed with the knowledge shared by the employees, I was able to start making some promises. I started with small promises. And then I grew those into more substantial commitments around areas requiring real change. Most importantly, I made sure that I delivered on the promises that I made.

Rather than making me look like a weak leader, this process of showing respect to earn respect helped demonstrate my commitment to resolving the challenges the team faced.

Earn Respect, Don't Expect It
Avoid falling into the trap of assuming your team will automatically want to follow your lead because of your new title. You will have to work hard to add value and earn respect.

BE PREPARED TO LEARN

"People feel good when they share and you listen."

WE HAVE JUST described the importance of gaining the trust of your team as early as possible in your new role. The concept of showing respect to earn respect is the first step in this process. Being prepared to actually learn from your team is the next critical component.

All members of your team have something valuable to contribute. It is your job to learn what that value is. As early as you can in your new role, spend the necessary time with all the members of your team to personally learn their perspectives on the business. Doing this will not only enhance their respect for you but also help you create an excellent road map with which to focus your first ninety days.

To learn the most from your team, it is best to ask thought-provoking, open questions that require more than one-word, yes-or-no answers. These questions create the opportunity for sharing ideas in a discussion, without the uncomfortable feeling of being interrogated.

To set the tone, you might say: "As I am new to my position, I would really like to learn more about your thoughts on the company." You can then go on to ask questions, such as: "What are the parts of your role you enjoy and don't enjoy? How would you describe the mood of the business? If you were doing my job, what would be the first three things you would do? What is the worst thing I could do?"

There is a positive emotional effect in encouraging people to share the things they would really like to tell you. People feel good when they share and you listen. By employing this approach, you'll obtain valuable knowledge about your business—the good, the bad, and the ugly—and especially about the people within it.

You might even pick up some quick wins to implement early on in your tenure—including the opportunity to credit those changes back to the individuals who first suggested them. This will enhance the trust and loyalty you earn, as few actions motivate more than public recognition for a good idea.

In one of my first general management roles, I was responsible for eighty people. As the first task in my new position, I set about meeting everybody face-to-face, personally. Each meeting lasted only about thirty minutes, but the information I gathered during each of those thirty-minute meetings was invaluable. In just one week's worth of meeting time, I gained knowledge acquired by my team's years of work experience. And I was able to learn firsthand—without preconception—just how every member of my team felt about the business. It was easily the most important week of my first year as general manager.

No new manager should miss this opportunity to learn from the team as they move out of the starting blocks in their new role.

Be Prepared to Learn

Create as much time as necessary to learn from your team through candid feedback in one-on-one sessions. It will be the most important time you spend as you start your new role.

MAKE THE TIME

"...one-on-ones help you get to the heart of problems quicker."

D EVELOPING AN EARLY understanding of the issues affecting your team is one of the most important objectives to achieve as you get started in a new management role. As we just explored, using one-on-one meetings is an effective way to do this; these meetings are not just an effective way to get started, however. Meaningful one-on-one time with each member of your team is an important management activity to continue on a regular basis. Mark Horstman, co-founder of Manager Tools LLC, considers it so important that he refers to one-on-one-meetings as "*the common thread of all exceptional managers.*"

Managers have used the phrase "my door is always open" for years, but unfortunately, this has become somewhat of a cliché and can, in fact, sound a lot more like "please don't bother me" than "I'm free to talk anytime." Despite the promise an open-door policy provides, it rarely encourages the type of discussion that managers need to have with their team members. If you only hold one-on-one discussions on an opportunistic basis, you will soon find that, as your schedule fills up, the meetings end up being dropped. And when you do hold them, there are so many things to cover that you end up hijacking the meeting with your own agenda rather than discussing the topics your team members want to talk about.

One-on-one time is an opportunity for a person to express their thoughts on a subject without the fear of interruption or disapproval from a colleague. As such, one-on-ones help you, as a manager, get to the heart of problems quicker. You will learn much more about the way your team members approach their jobs, the company, and the problems they face. Your team will start to learn more about the way you think and how you approach problems, which will pay dividends down the road—for you and them. The interest you show in one-on-ones will even help motivate the members of your team. With individual issues tackled separately, you will be free to focus on topics that affect the team as a whole, improving the effectiveness and efficiency of your team meetings as well.

There are some simple principles to ensuring effective one-on-one sessions.

Schedule regular time proactively. Depending on how many direct reports you have and the nature of your position, schedule a fixed, weekly time to meet with each member of your team. You could choose to hold one to two sessions each day. Alternatively, some managers prefer to set aside one day in the week for all catch-ups so that everyone knows that, for example, Monday is your day for one-on-ones.

Don't let it become a burden. There will be times when something unavoidable that clashes with the meeting comes up. If, for a good reason, the meeting needs to be rearranged, that's OK. But don't let cancellations start to become a habit. Flexibility is a good thing, and your team will thank you for it, but, equally, they will appreciate your diligence in setting time aside for them on a regular basis.

Make it their meeting. It is their meeting to discuss anything they want. Let them set the agenda. Of course you will thread in your own topics as part of the discussion, but this is primarily their uninterrupted hour with you to share what is affecting their work life and how they feel about it. Your job is to listen and, if need be, provide the guidance required to work through the issues.

You will be surprised at what you can learn by spending a weekly, one-on-one hour with each member of your team.

Make the Time

Do more than declare an open-door policy in your office. Actually make the time to hold individual meetings with each of your team members on a regular basis, and let them set the agenda.

PERSONALIZE MOTIVATION

"...members of your team will each respond differently to the motivational techniques you use."

I F YOUR GOAL is to inspire others, not just manage them, we recommend you spend time thinking about the individual members of your team and the best ways available for you to contribute to their motivation at work. While there are many well-known and effective methods for motivating people to perform, there's no magic formula that works for all people all the time.

Three methods that we feel are important when motivating individual members of your team are how you create a sense of purpose, how you help people develop, and how you come across to the people around you. Each will have a significant impact on how successful you are in motivating others.

Create a sense of purpose. Teams come together and perform as one unit when they are working toward a common goal or trying to overcome a common challenge. You can identify what these are for your team and build a strong sense of identity around them. But we recommend you make it personal—down to the individual level—by helping each person in your team identify what they feel is the true purpose of their role. What do they think their contribution is to the wider team effort? How would they like to create impact? What do they find most interesting and compelling about their job? Give them the opportunity to describe these in their own words. You can use this information in your one-on-one sessions to relate achievements back to each team member's self-described sense of purpose.

Encourage personal and professional development. Many people equate their sense of satisfaction to the degree to which they have learned, gained, or developed while performing their work rather than simply the impact they've had on the results of the business. Tapping into people's innate desire to grow and develop in their careers is an effective way to motivate high performance. To do this, you can try to create opportunities for someone who enjoys a particular aspect of their job to become more deeply immersed in it—even if the knowledge they acquire may sometimes go beyond what is needed to perform their role. The more someone learns in their role, the better they become at performing it, and the more they want to develop that ability further. The pursuit of expertise can create a virtuous circle in which both the business and the individual benefit.

Be aware of your impact. As the manager, your motivational levels will have an effect on your team. Even if you are not always aware of it happening, the people who work for you are monitoring your body language, mood, and behavior. Like it or not, this can have a direct impact on their morale. When you first step into management, it can be difficult to keep yourself looking positive and motivated, but you need to be conscious of how you come across to others. You don't need to pretend to be superhuman. Your team will see through this. Just be aware that, as the leader of the team, your good mood can be infectious and your bad mood contagious.

The members of your team will each respond differently to the motivational techniques you use. Regardless of the approach you choose, make sure you personalize it to focus on their sense of purpose and desire to develop in their roles.

Personalize Motivation

Don't just manage your team; inspire them. Help individuals discover their sense of purpose in a role, encourage their development personally and professionally, and make sure you understand the impact your personal motivation will have on them.

ALLOW THE FREEDOM TO FAIL

"Creating the freedom to fail is essential, and your ability to embrace it will set you apart from most other newly appointed managers."

BEING ON TOP of things, running a tight ship, and delivering consistently is one thing. Scrutinizing every act, being involved in every decision, and insisting on approval at every juncture is quite another. Balancing your need to own your team's deliverables with your team's desire for a sense of freedom at work is an important equilibrium for every manager to reach. Sometimes this requires you to step far enough back to give your team the freedom to fail.

While it may lead to occasional mistakes, we are not advocating missed deadlines or poor results. What we're advocating is an approach that will help create confident teams prepared to make quick, sensible decisions when needed, yet ready to seek help when required. Creating the freedom to fail is essential, and your ability to embrace it will set you apart from most other newly appointed managers.

Of course this requires you to employ people you can trust. As business author Jim Collins once said, "*The moment you feel the need to tightly manage someone, you've made a hiring mistake.*" We'll address how to avoid hiring mistakes later on in the book, but what we like most about this quote is how it demonstrates the importance of delegating responsibility to talented, well-trained individuals.

Here are some thoughts on how you can allow the freedom to fail.

Allow decisions to be made as far down the reporting line as possible. Set decision-making guidelines, be clear about priorities, and be consistent about what is acceptable and what is not. Then give your team the freedom to act within these parameters, including enough freedom to make mistakes. Praise good decisions by your employees. When decisions go badly, be as supportive as possible in the process to make things right. Hold people accountable for their actions rather than rushing to adjust the limits of authority or to reverse decisions made by employees. In an environment where people feel their decisions are respected and they have accountability for their actions, they will more readily recognize when a decision might require management involvement.

Encourage the members of your team to set their own objectives. Before preparing top-down, stretch targets for your team, first ask them to suggest their own objectives. Ask them to set an aggressive but realistic goal. By doing this, you encourage your team to give real consideration to their targets by providing them with ownership and accountability. Ownership and accountability can be great motivators. And, believe it or not, the targets that come back from your team will often be higher than what you would have set yourself. You can then even shave a bit off their numbers to create the positive pressure of making them feeling obligated to hit a target that even you, the boss, has lowballed.

Work relentlessly to remove barriers to performance. When limits of authority are constraining and managers second-guess every decision that comes from below them in the hierarchy, companies become plagued by inaction. Break down these barriers to create a bias toward taking action. Ask your team to openly discuss barriers and enablers with you. Do your best to be aware of any internal processes that may be inhibiting action or changes that could be enacted to improve efficiency. Help remove barriers and help create more enablers—do all you can to help your team go further and faster.

By ensuring decisions are made as close to the coal face as possible and that objectives are influenced by those who own them, you will create a greater sense of ownership and accountability. A team that feels a sense of ownership—and is held accountable for its actions—will also feel a greater motivation to deliver results.

Allow the Freedom to Fail

Ownership and accountability are tremendous motivators. Instead of dictating every action and objective, allow decisions to be made further down the chain, work to remove the barriers that hinder your team's performance, and be tolerant of inevitable mistakes.

BECOME A COACH

"....if the only time someone in your team hears about an issue is once a year, there is something wrong with the way you are coaching."

ALLOWING PEOPLE THE freedom to fail is very different to being tolerant of continuous mistakes. If someone really strays beyond acceptable limits, you do, of course, need to take action. One of your responsibilities as a manager is to help people improve in their roles and surpass their own expectations of what they thought they could achieve. Terry Leahy, the former CEO of Tesco Plc., described this best when he said, *"Leadership is about helping people go further than they think they can go on their own."*

Many organizations conduct annual appraisals, but, if the only time someone in your team hears about an issue is once a year, there is something wrong with the way you are coaching. Coaching is best done frequently and as close to the event as possible. It should comprise positive reinforcement of activities you want to see more often, not just constructive criticism.

Here are some ideas to help you.

Make the feedback timely and confidential. Whenever possible, give constructive feedback immediately after the event (or as close to the event as possible). The longer you wait to share feedback, the more it will feel like discipline and the less it will feel like coaching. Remember, coaching is best provided one-on-one in an environment where your team members can feel as comfortable as possible about the discussion. Choose the timing and the location of your feedback carefully. These factors play an important role in the effectiveness of your coaching.

Use the traffic-light technique. When providing feedback, instead of only focusing on behaviors that need to stop (red) and areas for improvement (yellow), be sure to also highlight behaviors that you'd like to see more often (green). In his book *The One-Minute Manager*, Kenneth Blanchard refers to the practice of "*catching people doing things right*" and it is a very effective part of coaching.

For example, if you are giving feedback after a client meeting you have attended, instead of just pointing out areas for improvement, you might say something like this:

"*You built great rapport in that meeting. It's a real strength of yours and a skill I'd like you to help me develop with others on the team [green]. Your presentation was strong, but you could take more time to dig a bit deeper on some of the client's issues before you start talking [yellow]. One thing you should remember is not to directly criticize competitors. I know it's tempting, but it can easily backfire [red]."*

Develop your own coaching skills. There is an entire industry dedicated to leadership coaching. Make use of these resources. Read books on the topic. Seek out your own professional management coach. Ask some of the more experienced managers in your business for recommendations. The more you expose yourself to different coaching techniques, the more you will develop your skills. Try them for yourself, and when you find something to be valuable, make it available to your team.

I've always enjoyed sharing my favorite books with aspiring managers in my team. After taking the time to explain why I found a particular book to be useful, I would hand it out to each member of my team, who would find a handwritten note from me inside the front cover. The impact was often significant—not just in terms of helping to improve performance and engagement but also because it conveyed my genuine interest in their career development. It's a meaningful and memorable practice that I've heard many of the team continued when they became managers themselves.

There is no one, fixed way to coach, and you'll develop your own approach over time. But if you keep your feedback timely, focus on catching people doing things right, and make the extra effort to continue developing your own coaching skills using outside resources, you will have made a much better start to coaching others than most managers ever do.

Become a Coach

Don't wait for the annual appraisal to share feedback. Make an effort to develop your own coaching skills, and make coaching a daily activity. Balance your constructive comments about things that need to change with positive feedback about behaviors that are worth commending.

BUILD CLOSER CONNECTIONS

"For you to be successful as a leader, your colleagues and your team have to want you to be successful."

MAKING A CONNECTION with people is not just about one-on-one coaching or spending time on the road together. It's about getting to know your colleagues as people. And it's about finding out what is really important to them—both at work and away from the office.

For you to be successful as a leader, your colleagues and your team have to want you to be successful. If they don't, you won't be. And it's difficult for people to want you to be successful if they don't feel you've made an effort to connect with them on a personal level. People want to feel that they matter. As a manager, you have the opportunity to help make that happen.

Building closer connections shouldn't be forced; it should be genuine. Here are a few tips to help you build closer connections without coming across as phony.

Take time to listen. Asking questions about someone's interests, not just work, is the most important first step in building personal rapport. Everyone you work with has a life outside of work, so make the effort to listen to what they are saying about it. Be interested, stay focused on the conversation, and resist the urge to interrupt someone else's story about a personal interest so that you can speak about yours.

Keep a notebook. Listening is critical, but recalling the information you've heard is also important. Recalling details about the people you work with may be easy enough when you have a small team, but the reality is that it will become frustratingly difficult as your team and network grow. A good habit to adopt is to keep notes of personal and professional details that you might otherwise forget. You will be grateful for the information when you are next due to meet someone whom you had an in-depth conversation with a year ago.

Show some respect. Everyone is busy, and everyone has pressing deadlines. But being stressed or in a hurry are not excuses for being rude. Being friendly and polite with your colleagues goes a long way to building rapport and preserving connections. And be polite not just *to* your colleagues but when you're *around* your colleagues as well. Being discourteous to staff at a restaurant or rude to subcontractors who clean your office is not only the wrong way to behave, it can also damage your credibility in the eyes of others.

I recall the CEO of one of the first businesses I worked in going on a client visit with me. During our taxi journey, I mentioned that my wife was considering making a career change. About a month later, I received an e-mail from him, and at the foot of the e-mail was, "PS—some help for your wife," in which he included links to some of his favorite books on life transitions—a simple and quick gesture for him but a really meaningful one for me.

Taking the time to listen to, and remember, information that is important to your colleagues is an important step in building the close personal connections that will make your job more enjoyable and fulfilling and, in turn, help you build a strong network. Take it seriously.

Build Closer Connections

Learn the skills required to build rapport with your colleagues, put them into practice by learning some important information about your workmates, and follow up with people on topics they are interested in.

LET OTHERS SPEAK

"...listening is not about waiting for an opportunity to speak."

MANAGERS ARE OFTEN people who speak well and are confident in front of others. The challenge of being good at something is that it is difficult to resist the urge to do it. As a result, many managers are all too often in a hurry to speak.

An essential part of your role as a leader is to know what is really going on inside your business. To do that effectively, you have to learn to listen. Good listening is not about waiting for an opportunity to speak. Good listening means that you only start speaking when you have done all you can to uncover the real thinking behind what you've heard. It means asking questions—lots of them—but in a way that does not make someone feel like you are simply interrogating them.

Good answers make you feel clever, but good questions make you wise. As Voltaire put it, "*Judge a person by his questions, not by his answers.*"

Here are some habits to develop that will help you focus on becoming a better listener, especially if you are one of life's natural talkers.

Use the three "Whys?". Resist the urge to immediately respond to a point that has been made. Rather, before you start giving your own input, try to ask "Why?" at least three times first. Very often, the first answer someone gives to a question is a reflection of some much deeper thought or opinion. If you simply respond to the first answer you get, you could miss the underlying thought. You need to keep digging with more questions rather than just starting to talk. Three "Whys?" really help you think about using your ears much more than your mouth, especially in the early stages of a conversation.

Expect a solution. A great norm to establish in your team is to insist that anybody who presents you with a problem needs to also come prepared with their thoughts on possible solutions. This not only helps encourage your team members to think, it also helps prevent you from just diving in to outline solutions and talking at someone, rather than listening to their perspective on the problem first.

Speak last. In a group setting, the dynamics are often different to those in a one-on-one setting. Team members might be more cautious about sharing opinions, and no one wants to look stupid in front of peers. So the tendency can be for several team members to stay quiet while the usual one or two more vocal characters dominate the airtime. To avoid this, work on getting everyone's views on a topic before you share your own. Give a voice to the silent majority, and ensure they say what they think without being drowned out by others—and before you influence their thinking too much with your own views.

Asking more questions has had a big influence on my management style. In the early days of my career, I used to jump right in to try and solve the problems of my team when they came looking for help. My enthusiasm to solve problems and take action led to numerous circumstances where a better solution existed (in the mind of my direct report), but I issued instructions on what we needed to do before anyone else had the opportunity to speak. When I finally learned to talk last and ask "Why?" at least three times to get to the bottom of the problem, I was able to determine that half the time the so-called problem wasn't even a problem after all. And when there was a real problem, finding the solution was easier than I had originally thought.

Let Others Speak

Keep asking "Why?" until you get to the truth behind an issue and develop the habit of drawing views out of others before you start sharing yours.

CONVERT COMPLEX TO SIMPLE

"...what people understand matters more than what you say."

CORPORATE LITERATURE IS often riddled with nonsense because managers choose to use complex language to demonstrate superior knowledge. Rather than thinking about whether their messages have been absorbed, they're thinking more about how clever they sound.

What does sounding clever have to do with being understood? Well, actually, nothing.

The most important thing to remember about clear communication is that what people understand matters more than what you say.

The temptation as a newly appointed manager may be to try and impress with complex language and long detailed e-mails to show you know your stuff. Avoid this pitfall. Instead choose simple and clear.

Here are three ideas to keep in mind when you communicate.

Give your conclusion up front. Present your main points at the beginning. Be it an e-mail, a slide deck, or a verbal presentation, people are far more likely to listen to what you have to say when they know what you are trying to say.

Strive for the Rule of Three. Time and again, research has shown that people prefer ideas and concepts with a maximum of three key points. Avoid ten-part plans or seven-step processes. Where you realistically can, stick to the Rule of Three.

Keep it short. A simple guideline to follow is to try and cut the length of any e-mail or presentation you prepare in half. Short sentences can have a lot more impact. Less is more and easier to remember.

He may not have had business leadership in mind when he said it, but Leonardo da Vinci could not have put it better: *"Simplicity is the ultimate sophistication."*

Convert Complex to Simple

Keep your language short and simple if you want to get your message across clearly.

PRESENT A STORY, NOT A SLIDE

"...turning on a laptop does not mean that we suddenly switch off our emotions."

THINK ABOUT THE number of slide presentations you've had to sit through in your working life. How many of these were truly memorable? Probably not many.

Most presentations fail to really engage people at a personal level. Managers assume that the best way to convey a message is with a display of facts and analysis. But conveying a message is not the same as winning an argument. And turning on a laptop does not mean that we suddenly switch off our emotions. The better way to convey a message—even a business message—is to ensure that the audience connects with the material in a personal way.

The facts do matter, and without them, any business presentation is destined to fall flat. But with the facts well in hand, if you want to get your underlying message through to your audience, your analysis needs to be included within a wider story. As story-telling expert Jonathan Gotschall explained, *"A story is a trick for sneaking a message into the fortified citadel of the human mind."*

Here are a few of our tips to help you sneak your message through.

Concentrate on the flow. When creating your presentation, spend as much time reviewing the transition from one slide to the next as you do creating the content for each slide. There should be a logical flow. As a test, flip through your slides quickly while only saying the main point of each slide. If you can tell your story coherently by doing this, your slide transitions are likely working well. If you can't, fix the flow.

Know the content. After ensuring the slides in your presentation flow from one to the next, you need to ensure that you are so familiar with the content that it is unnecessary for you to read the slides while giving the presentation. If you ever find yourself saying, "What this slide is saying is…" then you will have immediately lost your audience. Know the content better than anyone else in the room, look at the audience when you're speaking, and only use the slides as a prompt to keep you focused on the main points.

Practice your delivery. Once you have a solid handle on the content, you will have the opportunity to practice your storytelling. This will help get your message across by keeping the audience interested and lightening the tone. Using metaphors that help create memorable connections to the story or contrasting either-or statements, like "innovate or die," can be powerful. Forcing the audience to consider their own answers to rhetorical questions or adding color to the content through anecdotes helps make the audience actually feel part of the presentation you're delivering. Perfecting these techniques will ensure the audience is concentrating on you rather than watching the clock and waiting for the next presenter to take the stage.

There is no substitute for solid content, but if you use our storytelling tips above to complement your high-quality material with an engaging delivery that flows from one point to the next, your message will have more impact and you will appear more charismatic.

Present a Story, Not a Slide

Complement the facts and analysis in your presentations with a story line that flows and a confident delivery reinforced by metaphors, contrasts, and anecdotes.

RESPECT THE SIMPLE TRUTH

"There is no quicker way to lose respect than to appear to be holding back information..."

PEOPLE FEEL RESPECTED and respond better when they know they are being told the truth.

Clearly there are sensitivities involved in management, and you often need to choose your words with care, but if you try to distort an unpleasant fact or shield an unpopular truth, your team will eventually see through you.

You may think that you risk being challenged in front of others or you will damage employee morale if you tell the whole truth. But an equally concerning danger for a new manager is the risk of losing the respect of the team.

There is no quicker way to lose respect than to appear to be holding back information or manipulating a situation for your own benefit. Some leaders who make a habit of skirting direct communications even start believing their own stories—a sure sign that they are losing touch with reality and their teams.

If something is confidential, say so. If a decision has been made but management still hasn't decided how to proceed, let them know. If the results are bad, don't pretend they're good. Deliver the truth to your team. They can handle it.

The real benefit of straight talk is that a team that knows you will speak to them as if they can handle the truth is more likely to support you when the going gets tough. Colleagues who know they can trust what you say are more likely to trust you with information that they have.

Think about the following when you're faced with communicating tough news.

Simplicity. Consider the simplest way to communicate the information that needs to be understood. Using simple communication avoids the risk of others thinking you are trying to hide hard facts through clever words.

Timing. Telling the truth does not mean that you have to automatically share bad news the moment you hear it. Use your judgment, and pick the appropriate time and forum to deliver your message.

Style. Don't add glossy words just to create a happier mood. You can highlight positives alongside negatives—that's fine—but make sure you genuinely believe in them and are not just trying to deflect attention. Say what you mean, and mean what you say.

You may think that telling the truth is such an obvious characteristic for any business leader with integrity that it is almost not worth a chapter dedicated to the subject. But in your career, you will be faced with many situations in which you will have to carefully consider how you word a message. Truth is the most fundamental and, often, most difficult part of leadership integrity. Don't distort it for expedience.

Respect the Simple Truth

Most people know when their manager is spinning them a line. Ensure the message is simple, the timing is right, and that you believe in what you are saying.

Deliver

KNOW THE BIG PICTURE

"... give yourself time and space to map out a long-term direction."

A FEW MONTHS INTO their new roles, many managers discover that their daily list of activities leaves little time for long-term thinking. They find themselves fighting fires and dealing with the day-to-day aspects of their job rather than keeping an eye on the big picture. While this is quite common, managers who sustain long periods of career success are able to avoid this pitfall.

Active leadership is about getting the right things done, not merely about being—or worse, just looking—busy. While being seen to take action is a good way to demonstrate that you're working hard in your new role, working tirelessly on the wrong activities is foolish. As American entrepreneur Jim Rohn once put it: *"Don't mistake movement for achievement. It's easy to get faked out by being busy. The question is: busy doing what?"*

Don't become a busy fool—a manager who works tirelessly on the wrong activities. Instead give yourself the time and space to map out a long-term direction.

When I first got started as a new manager, I was so eager to dive into the daily tasks that I was completely unaware I ran the risk of losing sight of what was really important. It wasn't until I was knee-deep in my to-do list, wondering how I ever got so busy, that a more experienced manager took a few moments of his time to suggest I take a step back. He reminded me that I needed to focus on the big goals so that I could eliminate unnecessary tasks from my to-do list. In hindsight, this was some of the best advice I have ever received.

But how do you keep your mind on the big picture without sacrificing your daily to-do list?

The first step is to make knowing the big picture an important priority and creating the necessary time in your workweek to really think properly about it. Don't be afraid to leave the office for this. Insightful ideas will often come to you when you are away from work. Have you ever had the experience of letting your mind wander while on a flight and then suddenly having a moment of inspiration? That's no accident. It is the result of being in an environment of forced downtime, where you're not being held hostage by your to-do list. It's simply hassle-free time for you to think about things. We recommend creating more of this time in your workweek.

Here are some ideas to help you along the way.

Read. Get into the habit of reading newspaper articles, blogs, or magazines about management, leadership, business, and entrepreneurship. Things you read will often be the spark you need to ignite new thinking. Or you may even find yourself just copying the ideas outright. Steal with pride, as many great business leaders have done before you.

Reflect. Block out a two- to three-hour time slot every week to reflect. While it may not always be possible, it is best if you can set this time aside to be outside of the office, in a space where you are unlikely to be interrupted. If it can't be three hours, make it two. If it can't be two, make it one. Ideally choose a place where you feel relaxed or inspired. Use it to think things through and plan important decisions. Make it a sacrosanct period of your week.

Record. Form the habit of making notes—preferably with visual aids, like mind maps, and in notebooks that you can reference. This process of creating your own logbook of ideas for the future is a cathartic one. It allows you to feel that you are building solid plans for the future, rather than just aimlessly musing. It will also ensure that you don't forget your great ideas when you need them.

The concept of read, reflect, and record will help you to focus your actions on what's important in the big picture. While you won't have seen (or solved) every problem during your reflection time, you will have at least armed yourself with the tools you need to address them when the time comes.

Know the Big Picture

Create time for yourself to think issues through and to plan for the future, making sure you escape the trappings of your normal work environment to read, reflect, and record your thoughts. Your best ideas rarely happen in the office.

PERFECT THE ART OF
GETTING THINGS DONE

"...plan a series of steps working backward from the date of the end goal to the current day."

ONCE THEY HAVE set goals and communicated them to every person in the team, one challenge that many new managers face is following a path to achieving the goals. This is true in our personal lives too. We might be inspired by an ambitious life objective, but when the adrenaline has faded and we return to our day-to-day activities, we often fail to take the steps to get anywhere close to the objective.

Getting things done is an art that, when mastered, can work magic on any department, business unit, or company. It is the reason why so many business books have been published about execution, why even a substandard strategy can still be successful, and, for that matter, why even the most incredible strategy could still fail.

Business is full of action plans, yet all too often, action plans get started and never finished.

There are several techniques to avoid falling into the trap of action-plan ineffectiveness. Unfortunately, one chapter in *57 Minutes* is not sufficient time for us to embark on a complete project-management training program. But one excellent technique we've used is to plan a series of steps working *backward* from the date of the end goal to the current day.

We first outlined this approach in *57 Minutes: All That Stands Between You and a Better Life* as a means to achieving life objectives. But it is equally applicable to your management goals as well. Getting things done doesn't have to be a complex mechanism. In fact, sometimes it is all just about having a simple, easy-to-follow plan that works backward from the end goal.

Here's how we use planning in reverse to manage action plans at work.

- Decide on the end goal.
- Assign one person to be accountable, even if it is a team effort—otherwise you end up with division of responsibility, and nothing gets done.
- Choose a realistic due date or deadline. Ideally you should ask the person responsible to commit to a date. This makes them feel accountable, not just to you but also to themselves.

- Outline each step needed to achieve the goal. Put the steps in sequential order, working in reverse from the end objective to the current day.
- Code each step red (not yet begun), yellow (in progress), or green (completed). And allow space for comments.

Make sure the list is regularly updated and circulated to everyone on the team. You will be amazed how a name next to a color-coded task within a mapped-out process will drive behavior.

Obviously the art of getting things done is more involved than simply color coding a few steps to complete a task. To be clear, what we're suggesting here is not a replacement for sophisticated project management when it is required. But having tools that take you and your team from idea to delivery is an essential responsibility of leadership, and you should invest time in finding the ones that work for you. To get started, we highly recommend you learn more about the tools outlined in David Allen's book *Getting Things Done: The Art of Stress-Free Productivity*.

Perfect the Art of Getting Things Done

Create action plans that ensure things get done. Use the technique of planning in reverse by working backward from the date of delivery to outline the steps to completion.

DON'T TRY TO BE THE SMARTEST PERSON IN THE ROOM

"The ability to turn something with inherent challenges into a workable new idea can be the difference that separates mediocre teams from exceptional ones."

NNOVATION AND CHANGE are essential to growing and maintaining successful businesses. But innovation and change are risky, and many organizations try very hard to avoid risk. They employ experienced managers responsible for analyzing ideas and uncovering each and every challenge they present. These managers appear smart because they're able to come up with long lists of problems to accompany any new idea. But an idea accompanied by a long list of challenges is not necessarily a bad idea. Good leaders acknowledge that problems exist, but they focus their efforts on finding solutions.

I used to work at a large, risk-averse organization. We had a saying there: "It takes a million yeses to get something new approved, but only one no to stop everything in its tracks." Unfortunately, we were stopping great initiatives from happening due to small, easily surmountable challenges.

The ability to turn something with inherent challenges into a workable new idea can be the difference that separates mediocre teams from exceptional ones.

Jack Welch, former CEO of General Electric, used to ask the simple question, "What is the fatal flaw?" as a way to encourage his people not to waste time with the easily mitigated risks. Jack's philosophy was that good ideas survive on their merits and die at the hands of a single fatal flaw—not as a result of the many smaller challenges that may present themselves along the journey to delivering the solution.

Resist the urge to get caught up in just the problems. The smart people around you may help you avoid major mistakes, but your role is to ensure that they don't grind the business to a halt. There is an old Chinese saying: "*Those who say it cannot be done should not interrupt those doing it.*" Teddy Roosevelt famously said much the same thing in 1910 with these words:

"*It is not the critic who counts, not the man who points out how the strong man stumbles, or where the doer of deeds could have done them better...the credit belongs to the man who is actually in the arena...who strives to do the deeds, his place shall never be with those cold or timid souls who did not know victory nor defeat.*"

Successful leaders don't allow minor challenges to get in the way of great initiatives. Learn to evaluate problems, but don't allow them to curtail your team's efforts toward fresh ideas. Don't equate sounding smart with finding problems. By focusing your energy on finding solutions, you may not *feel* like the smartest person in the room, but in the end, you will enjoy more success.

Don't Try to Be the Smartest Person in the Room

Trying to sound smart is often a catalyst for just focusing on the problems. Instead look for solutions, and don't worry about who appears to be the smartest person in the room.

HIRE PEOPLE WHO WILL BE BETTER THAN YOU

"...nines and tens hire nines and tens, while fives and sixes hire threes and fours."

FEAR OFTEN LEADS to poor decision making. The fear of rejection, for example, may make a salesman reluctant to ask a customer for the order when the opportunity to close the deal presents itself. Fears like this—or as we like to call them, "crippling fears"—can be detrimental to your success as a manager. One common way in which crippling fears manifest themselves at work is the fear of being bettered by someone on your team. When this happens to people in management positions, it often leads to the poor practice of hiring low performers.

Don't go down this route. Remember: nines and tens hire nines and tens, while fives and sixes hire threes and fours. In other words, managers of a high caliber surround themselves with other people of high caliber. Good hiring practices are the backbone of strong company performance. The recruiting and hiring process is what brings in the talent, and it is your job as a leader to seek out this top talent and get them into your organization.

In our first book, *57 Minutes: All That Stands Between You and A Better Life*, we talk about one particular way to push through your fears by replacing your crippling fears with motivational ones. Replace the fear you may have of being overtaken in your career with the fear of mediocre team performance or the fear of becoming complacent in your work. These more motivating fears will help you overcome any tendency you may have to under-hire for important positions that report to you.

Always hire the best talent you can find. It elevates team performance on all levels. It keeps you on your toes. It shows your employees that you value top performance and actively seek top-quality people for your team. And it drives the performance of your team as a whole, ensuring good results and a genuine desire for continuous improvement.

Hiring people who will be better than you will actually boost your career, not threaten it. We have never seen managers who have hired highly talented people suffer from their decisions. They almost always end up reaping the benefits—not just in the performance of their team but also in their own promotion prospects. Having a team of nines and tens waiting to take over makes it much easier for the company to find new leadership opportunities for you. It is much more difficult for the company to provide you these opportunities if your team is full of threes and fours.

Think about it this way: if businesses are only as good as the people working in them and those working in them are always trying to hire people who are better than they are, the result has to be that the business improves. "*If each of us hires people who are better than we are, we shall become a company of giants,*" said advertising genius David Ogilvy. Being responsible for helping your organization become a company of giants can only be good for you in the long run.

Hire People Who Will Be Better than You
Only hire the best person you can find for the job. Strive to find people who are—or will be eventually—better than you.

TREAT RECRUITMENT AS A SCIENCE

*"...your ability to recruit effectively will help determine
your success over time."*

SETTING YOUR SIGHTS high and recruiting people who will be better than you is the right principle to follow. Making it happen, however, can be difficult. Despite the challenges, your ability to recruit effectively will help determine your success over time.

While the recruitment process will already be fairly established in many large companies, the role of getting the highest caliber of people into your organization is every manager's responsibility. In fact, leaving this responsibility solely to the HR department is a mistake. Recruitment should be a process in which the quantity and quality of candidates is directly influenced by your actions.

Here are some techniques to help you along.

Build a network of recruiters, proactively. Unless your company has already established its relationship with outside recruiting firms, you are likely to get approached by a lot of recruitment agents eager for your business. We suggest building your own network of recruiters that you've interviewed and selected proactively. Meet them face-to-face, and judge them on their ability to understand your requirements. Negotiate fees, but don't nickel-and-dime. Preserve a positive relationship. Then when the moment comes to recruit, mobilize this mini army of recruiters and wait for the candidates to come in.

Don't underestimate the importance of the job description. The more specific you are about the skills, attitude, and experience required, the more likely you are to get a high-quality response of suitable candidates. It is very important that the job description actually defines the candidate you want. Run it by more experienced managers in your business, and make sure you understand the difference between the must-haves and the nice-to-haves. The job description is your guide—the closer it matches the ideal candidate for the job, the better guide it will be. Don't pad the job description with required qualifications if you don't need them. And don't leave them out if you do.

Learn to read résumés effectively. It is extremely difficult to get a feel for a job candidate simply by reviewing their résumé, but this is the first gateway for almost all job applications, and good managers need to develop a keen eye for résumé review. One technique that we use is a "key word review." After reading a résumé for the first time, read back through it, scanning vertically to see if you can spot the key words for that role. For example, if you are recruiting for salespeople, see how many times the words "sales," "targets," or "pipeline" appear. You will be surprised how often a résumé supposedly positioning a candidate for a specific function actually contains very few references to activities that relate to that function. This can be a strong signal about the real desire of the candidate to fulfill the role.

Set some objective criteria for the interview. This is especially needed if several of your colleagues will also interview a candidate. Use the job description as a guide to create a list of criteria, and ask each interviewer to score against these. After the interviews have been conducted, you can score, compare, and discuss the candidates using these criteria. This helps avoid the situation in which the first person to give their opinions inadvertently influence the others. An objective set of criteria based on the job description helps to keep people true to their original opinions and serves as a great sanity check that the candidate has the skills needed rather than just being likeable in an interview.

Perfect your skills as an interviewer. Many statistics are available that demonstrate how difficult it is to find the right candidates using traditional résumé and interview techniques. Yet for most positions filled, these are still the main techniques being used. Therefore, it is important to perfect your skills as an interviewer, and we highly recommend making use of all available resources. When you interview candidates, you will be thinking about their experience, background, and education. But we suggest you also remember the three As:

- Attitude: do they have a strong sense of determination and direction?
- Aptitude: are they bright, confident, and focused, with the skills to do the job?
- Acceleration: can you imagine them having a rapid career progression?

And don't forget that, in an interview, you are marketing to the candidates as well. Top-talent applicants generally have options, so do not assume the selection process is a one-way street.

Recruiting is one of the headaches of management. You will sometimes get it wrong, but if you use these principles and turn recruiting into more of a science that complements your gut feeling, you will increase your chances of success significantly.

Treat Recruitment as a Science

Establish a clear process for recruiting rather than relying on opportunistic hires. Build a network of recruiters you trust, spend time on job profiles and résumés, and judge candidates against objective criteria, not just your gut feeling.

DON'T DELAY THE INEVITABLE

"A delayed problem only becomes more difficult to solve."

ONE OF THE hardest and most important things you will ever do is to remove an underperforming member from your team. Emotion can obscure what may seem like an obvious course of action, and new managers can struggle to follow through on decisions because of the self-doubt that accompanies inexperience.

Taking quick action to remove underperformers is critical. Making the decision to remove an underperformer from your team should not be taken lightly, however. There are many aspects to take into consideration, including work history, severance packages, company policies, and employment law, to name a few.

When faced with the challenge of having to let go of an underperformer, consider the following.

Is the performance problem an issue of attitude or aptitude? Understanding the nature of the performance problem is very helpful when determining what the best solution might be. The correct course of action for someone who has an attitude problem because, for example, they are unhappy that you were selected to take on the management role instead of them is very different to the course of action you might take for a person who just can't handle the requirements of the job. Before making any decisions on what needs to happen, spend the necessary time determining the nature of the problem—is it attitude, aptitude, or something else?

Can the performance problem be solved another way? Often, poor performance is not simply the fault of the person who is performing badly. Maybe the training was inadequate, maybe there is confusion in the job responsibilities, maybe there is a significant process problem and even the highest-caliber person would fail. As a manager, it is important to assess the situation objectively. If there is a way to remedy the problem without firing the person, it is always worth assessing. A few things you might want to consider include:

- Creating a performance plan—performance plans are designed with the employee to more closely manage desired performance. They are an important step in understanding the cause of underperformance.
- Transferring the person to another department where they may be a better fit—sometimes a person is just in the wrong job and there's a perfectly suitable position for them elsewhere in the company.
- Improving a system or a process—often the performance problem is simply not the person's fault and even the

most brilliant performers could fail. It is worth understanding the processes required to fulfill the job responsibilities. Maybe the issue is somewhere else and a simple process change could fix it.

Would you hire this person again? One of the most useful tools to use as the final tipping point in an underperformance situation is the would-you-hire-again test. This question forces you to think about whether the individual in question is someone you would want on your team if you imagined that their time in the job so far has been one long interview. A team member who has proven he or she is not up to the job over an extended period of time should really not have any greater right to be in the team than a candidate who failed to impress at the interview stage. If anything, the decision for the existing employee is based on a lot better evidence.

These decisions are rarely easy, but if you follow these tips and feel certain that letting the person go is the only option, then procrastination will not help. A delayed problem only becomes more difficult to solve. It is time to take action. Do not let your emotions cloud your judgment, and be fair and honest in how you proceed.

Don't Delay the Inevitable

When trying to decide if you should let someone go, first try to understand the underlying reasons for the poor performance and whether there are other options available to fix it. Finally, ask yourself whether you would have offered them a job in the first place if you knew then what you know now.

HAVE THE COURAGE TO COOPERATE

*"Politics will never disappear from business, but having
the courage to cooperate will set you apart from other managers."*

THE MOST EFFECTIVE businesses are those able to create an environment where the people within its walls are motivated to work together to perform. But with people come politics. And since you can't have a company without people, you can't have a company without politics.

While politics are an inherent part of every organization, the best leaders avoid being consumed by them. They demonstrate the courage to cooperate and the character to rise above company politics.

Managers are regularly faced with handling disputes where one manager takes a firm stance against another manager equally steadfast. The good manager in the room will help find a solution that benefits the organization as a whole—recognizing that there isn't necessarily a solution that will satisfy both teams. This may sound naïve, but in fact, if you relinquish your own short-term interests for the good of the company, it will not go unnoticed.

Of course situations arise where one high-potential manager is prepared to drop the partisan political game but their counterpart is simply less inclined to cooperate. Here are some tips to help you dump the departmental politics.

Put yourself in the shoes of the other department. Ensure you fully understand the situation from their perspective. The more you can appreciate their challenges, the more you'll see why the argument exists. Ask yourself how you would approach the argument if your bonus were based on their targets.

Position the situation as a challenge to resolve together. Avoiding team disputes is often all in the way it is presented. If you present the situation as a problem to resolve jointly, as opposed to a threat or challenge to the other team, it is more likely that your counterpart will be willing to talk.

Prepare your own compromise. Be ready to suggest a way forward that shows your good intentions for the organization; don't just argue blindly on behalf of your department. See the good points of your counterpart, and be prepared to commit to something for the sake of a reasonable compromise.

A duo of books published by the Arbinger Institute, *Leadership and Self-Deception* and *The Anatomy of Peace*, explains how to develop the character to cooperate with others for success. They illustrate how to avoid the natural instinct of holding preconceived ideas about others' intentions or seeing the world purely through your own eyes. We highly recommend them as a guide to rising above the politics.

Managers who struggle to resolve departmental politics are forced to implement strict rules of authority and escalation policies. Ultimately these restrain and demoralize people. Managers who coach people to have the courage to rise above the departmental politics and present real solutions will ultimately help improve the overall performance of their business and their own career prospects.

Ultimately this is a question of personal character. Politics will never disappear from business, but having the courage to cooperate will set you apart from other managers. As American military general Norman Schwarzkopf once said: *"Leadership is a potent combination of strategy and character. But if you must be without one, be without the strategy."*

Have the Courage to Cooperate

Real leaders have the courage to rise above departmental politics to create solutions that are right for the business as a whole.

MANAGE UP TOO

"...think about the things that you would like to see from the people who report to you."

MANAGEMENT IS NOT all about what goes on inside your own team. While the majority of your management time and effort will be dedicated to the people who report to you, managing up is also an important aspect of leadership.

Managing up is about learning how to manage your boss to ensure that they give you the space you need to do your work effectively. It is also about proactively ensuring that your relationship with your boss remains a positive one.

Understanding the techniques required to effectively manage your boss are quite simple. Just think about the things that you would like to see from the people who report to you. Simply put, managing up is as much about common sense as it is about following the rules.

Here are a few tips to help guide you.

Don't surprise your boss. Surprises in business are rarely good. Investors don't like them, and bosses don't like them. Keep your boss in the loop, and share bad news early. This gives your boss the opportunity to prepare for the possible scenarios and consider contingency plans to handle any backlash or problems that may occur. And when you're exposed to senior people in the business, prepare well for the meetings. Help demonstrate that there is an atmosphere of great teamwork rather than announcing something new that may catch your boss unaware.

Carry out the agreed plan. Support is an important thing when you're a boss. To get things done, you need everyone pulling in the same direction. It is OK to disagree with your boss and even good to push back with ideas of your own. What is not good, however, is to decide on your own that you will take a different course of action after something else has been decided. Not only will this result in a surprise (i.e., break rule number one), it will also create trust issues. Don't deviate from the plan without a discussion.

Share results, not just complaints. The last thing your boss wants to hear is a long list of all the problems you have encountered along the way to getting something done. It's fine to share issues, but not if that is the only thing you ever share. As business relationship expert Harry Mingail points out, *"Your boss is less interested in the storms you encountered than whether you brought in the ship."*

All three of these tips have a foundation in trust and good communication. You need to genuinely believe in your boss's judgment for the rules above to work. If for some reason you actually don't trust your boss and don't agree with the direction they are taking you in, it's time to think about your position and possibly look for other opportunities. Faking support is not sustainable over the long term.

Manage Up Too

Don't forget to manage up as well as down. Communicate effectively to garner trust. Don't surprise your boss, and do what you can to make your boss look good in front of his or her boss.

THINK SLOW BUT ACT FAST

"Once you've made your mind up and prepared the message to communicate, it is time to take action"

ONE CHARACTERISTIC THAT separates a good leader from a mediocre one is having the ability to know when a tough decision needs to be made and the strength to carry it out. However, being a good decision maker does not mean that you always need to make quick decisions. Sometimes waiting for more information is the right thing to do. Being a good decision maker means you make sensible decisions and then act on them in the manner and timing most appropriate to the situation.

A significant number of managers, especially novices, make quick decisions for the sake of appearing decisive. They may want to demonstrate their authority in front of their team. Or they may want their boss to see that they're a get-things-done kind of manager. Often new managers make snap decisions, act on them, and then are too embarrassed to step back and admit they made a mistake. Psychologist Daniel Kahnemann exposes just how poor our ability to make consistently good snap decisions is in his book *Thinking Fast and Slow*. It summarizes the systems the human mind uses to make choices and how important it is to make use of slow thinking. If you're interested in understanding more about the psychology behind this, we highly recommend giving it a read.

Only you can work your way through the thought process for each tough decision, but, when faced with one, consider the following.

Don't feel the need to rush. Make decisions only when you have thought the issues through and not just at the earliest point in time. Set criteria to help you evaluate your decisions. Listen to your gut, yes, but don't rely on it to the exclusion of everything else or assume that your gut feeling outweighs clear evidence that suggests a contrary view. As part of the decision-making process, include time to prepare the communication plan that goes with it. Decisions are not implemented in a vacuum, and if the decision has tough consequences, then effective and empathetic communication will play a significant part in ensuring the support you'll need to carry it out.

Evaluate multiple points of view. When you make decisions, don't just see the outcome through your own eyes. Imagine what you would think of the decision if you were, for example, the largest shareholder in the business. What might a completely neutral bystander say if you were explaining your logic to them? In other words, step outside your own bubble, and try hard to work through the implications for the wider company and stakeholders. Force yourself to see things from a minimum of three different perspectives—your own, the company's, and that of an objective onlooker.

Make it happen. Once you've made your mind up and prepared the message to communicate, it is time to take action. Being methodical about the decision-making process does not justify procrastinating the implementation. After making a tough decision, don't let the implementation plan fizzle out. Be willing to make adjustments as things proceed, but follow the plan through to the end. You put it in place for a reason. Postponing taking action on difficult decisions that you've already made will only make the problem worse.

Strong leaders don't shy away from tough decisions. They dedicate the appropriate amount of time and thought required, they put the necessary communication plan in place, and then they take action. Postponing a decision for more information is often the right thing to do. Postponing action after you've made a decision is almost always the wrong thing to do. Think slow then act fast.

Think Slow but Act Fast

Don't avoid the unpopular decisions. Perform the analysis properly, and once you have made the decision, act swiftly and follow the plan to completion.

HIT THE NUMBERS

"...the ultimate test of success is achieving results."

A S YOU SET about building your personal leadership style, the one non-negotiable characteristic you will need to include is a discipline for hitting the numbers. It is never easy, and there are always external factors that get in the way, but your discipline for achieving your targets must be unrelenting. The pursuit of soft skills is not a substitute for achieving hard results—the two must go hand in hand. Or, as Jim Rohn once put it: *"Discipline is the bridge between goals and achievement."*

The following tips will help you maintain focus on the targets.

Make it obvious that you care about results. Constantly measure whether the right things are being done to get you where you need to go, but remember, do not micromanage. Review the numbers that matter, and ask your team questions about them. Let them know that you have your eye on the ball.

Do the hard work. There really is no substitute for putting in the hard work. Do not assume that you can step back once things seem to be going in a successful direction simply because you have teams delivering on your plans. As Andy Grove, former CEO of Intel, once said: "*Success breeds arrogance; arrogance breeds complacency; complacency breeds failure. Only the paranoid survive.*" Be paranoid about achieving your results, and do the necessary hard work.

See things through. Be consistent with your own task management and finishing things off. Managers who declare new initiatives with a fanfare and then seem to never mention them again are viewed as fickle. Send the message that you commit to finishing what you start and expect the same from your team.

Whatever the nature of the new skills you have picked up by reading this book—developing people, taking time to think of the big picture, communicating well, motivating your team, making hiring decisions, and so on—the intention is for these skills to help you achieve success as a new manager. And the ultimate test of success is achieving results.

Hit the Numbers

Be an enlightened manager who hits the numbers, not just an enlightened manager.

TREAT FAILURE AS A VACCINE

"...your ability to recover and learn from failure will define your eventual success almost more than anything else."

SPEAK WITH ANYONE who has ever missed a target, lost a talented employee or failed to hire one, missed out on a commercial opportunity, seen a competitor win a deal, or delivered a presentation that flopped. They will all tell you that getting over it and moving on was incredibly difficult.

Failure may seem to be a strange topic for the concluding chapter of a book about becoming a better leader, but it is important to consider because failure in a management position is different than failure in an individual-contributor role. The stakes are higher, more people are affected, and you are under continuous observation by your team and others. For managers, recovering from failure is essential.

This is what we recommend you keep in mind when recovering from failure.

Be honest. Do not try to cover up your tracks and pretend nothing bad has happened. And definitely do not try to pass the blame to someone else. Your failure will come to light, and when it does, it will seem ten times worse if others think that you were trying to avoid your responsibility or lay the blame on some unsuspecting colleague.

Toughen up. Show your grit, and accept that something disappointing has happened—what doesn't kill you does make you stronger. Although it most likely will not come naturally, one of the best ways to recover from a failure is hard work. Weak leaders disengage; strong leaders double their efforts.

Take notes. Analyze what went wrong, get input from others, and make a written note to help you learn from your mistake. You can call it your "screw-up list: bad mistakes and how to avoid making them again." It will require a bit of that grit we talked about earlier, but getting feedback from others and keeping a tally of your mistakes can be therapeutic. It really helps.

Push through. After admitting to the mistake, dealing with the fallout, and understanding how to avoid the same mistake next time, it is time to get on with it. Don't wallow in self-pity. You have too much work to do to be hung up on one mistake.

Embrace risk. Although failure often comes from attempting something new, the worst thing you can do is to stop taking risks. Don't let a mistake in the past make you shy away from your next challenge. As Einstein once said, "*The surest way never to fail is never to try something new*." That's just not an option.

I recall early in my sales career that I had a particularly bad quarter. It was a horrible feeling. The easiest thing would have been to make excuses and blame market conditions. Instead I took the advice of a more experienced colleague who told me that the best salespeople take the hit, figure out what went wrong with their own performance, and then double their efforts. That is exactly what I did. I built a healthier pipeline, changed my approach in certain areas, and just got on with it. The following quarter I was significantly over target and had the best sales run of my career.

Thomas J. Watson, the second president of IBM, once said, "*If you want to increase your success rate, double your failure rate.*" Managers the world over have found solace in this famous quote because failure truly is the vaccine with which we immunize ourselves against the future. You can't avoid failure. But your ability to recover and learn from failure will define your eventual success almost more than anything else.

Treat Failure as a Vaccine

Failure happens to everyone: be honest about it when it happens, learn from it, pick yourself up, and increase your work rate. The people who are best at recovering from failure normally make the best leaders.

BRINGING IT ALL TOGETHER

Hopefully you have now picked up practical ideas that you can implement straight away in your new management role. You can dip in and out of this book when you need to—it is not an exercise in memory. To make things simpler, let's recap the summary points from each chapter into a short cheat sheet.

Inspire

Earn Respect, Don't Expect It: *Avoid falling into the trap of assuming your team will automatically want to follow your lead because of your new title. You will have to work hard to add value and earn respect.*

Be Prepared to Learn: *Create as much time as necessary to learn from your team through candid feedback in one-on-one sessions. It will be the most important time you spend as you start your new role.*

Make the Time: *Do more than declare an open-door policy in your office. Actually make the time to hold individual meetings with each of your team members on a regular basis, and let them set the agenda.*

Personalize Motivation: *Don't just manage your team; inspire them. Help individuals discover their sense of purpose in a role, encourage their development personally and professionally, and make sure you understand the impact your personal motivation will have on them.*

Allow the Freedom to Fail: *Ownership and accountability are tremendous motivators. Instead of dictating every action and objective, allow decisions to be made further down the chain, work to* remove the barriers that hinder your team's performance, and be tolerant of inevitable mistakes.

Become a Coach: *Don't wait for the annual appraisal to share feedback. Make an effort to develop your own coaching skills, and make coaching a daily activity. Balance your constructive comments about things that need to change with positive feedback about behaviors that are worth commending.*

Build Closer Connections: *Learn the skills required to build rapport with your colleagues, put them into practice by learning some important information about your workmates, and follow up with people on topics they are interested in.*

Let Others Speak: *Keep asking "Why?" until you get to the truth behind an issue and develop the habit of drawing views out of others before you start sharing yours.*

Convert Complex to Simple: *Keep your language short and simple if you want to get your message across clearly.*

Present a Story, Not a Slide: *Complement the facts and analysis in your presentations with a story line that flows and a confident delivery reinforced by metaphors, contrasts, and anecdotes.*

Respect the Simple Truth: *Most people know when their manager is spinning them a line. Ensure the message is simple, the timing is right, and that you believe in what you are saying.*

Deliver

Know the Big Picture: *Create time for yourself to think issues through and to plan for the future, making sure you escape the trappings of your normal work environment to read, reflect, and record your thoughts. Your best ideas rarely happen in the office.*

Perfect the Art of Getting Things Done: *Create action plans that ensure things get done. Use the technique of planning in reverse by working backward from the date of delivery to outline the steps to completion.*

Don't Try to Be the Smartest Person in the Room: *Trying to sound smart is often a catalyst for just focusing on the problems. Instead look for solutions, and don't worry about who appears to be the smartest person in the room.*

Hire People Who Will Be Better than You: *Only hire the best person you can find for the job. Strive to find people who are—or will be eventually—better than you.*

Treat Recruitment as a Science: *Establish a clear process for recruiting rather than relying on opportunistic hires. Build a network of recruiters you trust, spend time on job profiles and résumés, and judge candidates against objective criteria, not just your gut feeling.*

Don't Delay the Inevitable: *When trying to decide if you should let someone go, first try to understand the underlying reasons for the poor performance and whether there are other options available to* *fix it. Finally, ask yourself whether you would have offered them a job in the first place if you knew then what you know now.*

Have the Courage to Cooperate: *Real leaders have the courage to rise above departmental politics to create solutions that are right for the business as a whole.*

Manage Up Too: *Don't forget to manage up as well as down. Communicate effectively to garner trust. Don't surprise your boss, and do what you can to make your boss look good in front of his or her boss.*

Think Slow but Act Fast: *Don't avoid the unpopular decisions. Perform the analysis properly, and once you have made the decision, act swiftly and follow the plan to completion.*

Hit the Numbers: *Be an enlightened manager who hits the numbers, not just an enlightened manager.*

Treat Failure as a Vaccine: *Failure happens to everyone: be honest about it when it happens, learn from it, pick yourself up, and increase your work rate. The people who are best at recovering from failure normally make the best leaders.*

RECOMMENDED READING LIST

Getting Things Done: The Art of Stress-Free Productivity, David Allen

Leadership and Self-Deception, The Arbinger Institute

The Anatomy of Peace, The Arbinger Institute

Good to Great, Jim Collins

The First 90 Days, Michael D. Watkins

Straight from the Gut, Jack Welch

The One Minute Manager, Ken Blanchard and Spencer Johnson

Management in 10 Words, Terry Leahy

Leadership Plain and Simple, Steve Radcliffe

Drive: The Surprising Truth About What Motivates Us, Dan Pink

Thinking Fast and Slow, Daniel Kahneman

Reinventing Organizations, Frederic Laloux

Hostage at the Table, George Kohlrieser

The Halo Effect, Phil Rosenzweig

ACKNOWLEDGMENTS

We would like to thank the following people for reviewing the contents of *Management in 57 Minutes*: Rafael Altavini, Sebastian Hill, Greg Hodge, Daniel Huber, James Ireson, Larry Jackson, Sarah Lever, and Tim Robson.

ABOUT THE AUTHORS

Mike and Pierre met at business school in Lausanne, Switzerland. They formed a firm friendship and eventually collaborated on their first book, *57 Minutes: All That Stands Between You and a Better Life*, a short-format self-help book that went on to be a Top 20 *Amazon* download.

Management in 57 Minutes is the second book in the *57 Minutes* series.

Mike has spent his life in pursuit of as many new experiences as possible and has enjoyed a career spanning multiple industries and international leadership roles. He currently lives in Canada with his wife, Cathy, and their two children. He works as an entrepreneur and management consultant helping to grow new ideas into operating businesses.

Pierre is CEO of a research business based in Asia and lives in Singapore with his wife, Sarah, and their three children. Pierre is an avid student of human behavior. Throughout his diverse career as a lawyer, business leader, and non-executive director, he has subscribed to the view that to live is to learn.

Printed in Great Britain
by Amazon.co.uk, Ltd.,
Marston Gate.